Sports
Rhymes
of
Soccer

Paul Auday

Illustrations by Ryan Kerrigan - Foreword by Bob Rigby

AuthorHouse™
1663 Liberty Drive
Bloomington, IN 47403
www.authorhouse.com
Phone: 833-262-8899

Because of the dynamic nature of the Internet, any web addresses or links contained in this book may have changed
since publication and may no longer be valid. The views expressed in this work are solely those of the author and do
not necessarily reflect the views of the publisher, and the publisher hereby disclaims any responsibility for them.

Any people depicted in stock imagery provided by Getty Images are models,
and such images are being used for illustrative purposes only.
Certain stock imagery © Getty Images.

This book is printed on acid-free paper.

ISBN: 978-1-6655-0808-7 (sc)
       978-1-6655-0809-4 (e)

Print information available on the last page.

Published by AuthorHouse 06/07/2022

authorHOUSE·

Dedication

This book is dedicated to my father, Jose Horacio Auday. My dad is from one of the greatest soccer countries in the world, Argentina, where he began his medical training to become a doctor. In his mid-twenties, he moved to the United States of America (USA) to complete his residency. He eventually settled in Philadelphia, Pennsylvania, where Dr. Auday provided more than fifty years of medical service, including his two-year tenure (1974-1975) with the Philadelphia Wings, a professional (pro) lacrosse team that competed in the original National Lacrosse League. In those same two years that Dr. Auday worked for the Wings at the Spectrum in Philadelphia, the National Hockey League's Philadelphia Flyers were crowned the Stanley Cup champions.

PHILADELPHIA WINGS
Executives & Staff

Dr. Maurice C. Tepper	Director of Medical Affairs
Dr. Jose Auday	Orthopedic Surgeon
Dr. Bernard Holloran	Associate Team Physician
Dr. Everett Borghesani	Oral Surgeon
Dr. Irv Paul	Dentist
Jay Seidman	Promotion Director
Joe Farber	Traveling Secretary
Dolores DiSanto	Ticket Manager
Rosemary Burns	Bookkeeper
Marsha Jean Rossi	Secretary

iv

Pennsylvania Medical Society
&
The Philadelphia County Medical Society

HONOR

Jose H. Auday, MD, FACS

In recognition of
Fifty Years of Medical Service

Faithfully performed in the traditional ideals of the medical profession

Presented on the twentieth day of June in the year 2003

President, Pennsylvania Medical Society

President, The Philadelphia County Medical Society

Contents

Foreword

As a boy growing up in suburban Philadelphia during the 1950s and 1960s, I was immersed in an athletic culture that included football, basketball, and baseball. The passing of the seasons was linked to the sports that I loved and participated in.

In the sixth grade, a high school physical education teacher in my school district introduced soccer to any interested boys in a spring intramural program, hoping to boost the number of seventh-grade boys willing to choose soccer as the sport they would play in middle school and high school. That intramural program was the beginning of a lifelong love affair with what Pelé — the world famous Brazilian soccer star who actually became a teammate of mine in 1976 while playing with the New York Cosmos — coined "The Beautiful Game."

Some memories I have during my soccer career include the following: being the first pick in the 1973 North American Soccer League (NASL) college draft; winning the 1973 NASL championship with the Philadelphia Atoms as a rookie; being the first soccer player to appear on the cover of *Sports Illustrated*; playing for the United States Men's National Team; and playing with international stars, such as Brazil's Pelé, Ireland's George Best, and the Netherlands' Johan Cruyff.

Over my thirteen-year soccer career, the foremost thing that stands out to me is the love, passion, enjoyment, and reverence that I have for the game of soccer, which is shared throughout the world.

Reading Paul's poems brought me back to the very heart and foundation of my love for and dedication to a game that is revered in every country on our planet.

Paul's poems took me back to my childhood memories of being introduced to a game that would be a prominent part of my life and continues to be.

The poems radiate the childlike passion, the wonderment, the reverence for the game, the teams, and the players who comprise the history of "The Beautiful Game" for its millions of fans.

I hope that you take these poems in with the spirit they were crafted and that they transport you, as they did for me, back to a time in your life when the game of soccer was becoming part of your very being!

— **Bob Rigby**

About Bob Rigby

Bob Rigby: The Goalkeeper Whose Star-Making Saves Raised the Profile of Soccer in America

On August 25, 1973, at Texas Stadium, in the North American Soccer League Final, it was a landmark moment for soccer when a great goalie, Robert Alan "Bob" Rigby Jr., made saves to help the expansion Philadelphia Atoms shut out the host Dallas Tornado 2-0, and in the air he sometimes seemed to magically hover;

So on September 3, 1973 — with the accompanying caption "SOCCER GOES AMERICAN" — the levitation-enhanced goaltending success of Philly's Bob Rigby earned him a place in history — as the first soccer player to ever appear on a *Sports Illustrated* cover!

Introduction

Soccer is the most popular sport in the world! In the United States of America, this sport is called *soccer* rather than its original name, *football*, in order to distinguish it from the American sport of football. But in most countries around the world, this superb sport is called **football**. In a single match between two teams, a player (forward, midfielder, defender, or goalkeeper) uses at least one **foot** to control/dribble/pass/shoot a **ball**, and the team that scores more goals wins.

As a kid growing up in suburban Philadelphia in the 1970s and 1980s, I played Pennsylvania youth soccer for the Penn Valley Mustangs, the 1980 champions of the Delco Soccer League in the Novice A (Under-12) Division. Six years later, I earned 1986 All-State honors in soccer while playing for Harriton High School of the Lower Merion School District, just outside of Philadelphia.

In the United States (U.S.), professional soccer has risen to much greater prominence in the 1990s and 2000s. *Sports Rhymes of Soccer* features five poems about the following subjects: the historic heroes of the FIFA World Cup*; the two FIFA Players of the 20th Century, Pelé and Diego Maradona; the connections between basketball and soccer; and the recent success of the United States Women's National Team in both the FIFA Women's World Cup and the Summer Olympic Games.

Many soccer awards and records appear in this book. Some of the earlier FIFA awards mentioned in the poems were given out retrospectively, but they are listed in the years in which they were earned. In addition, there are three kinds of World Cup records cited in this book: men's, women's, and *overall* World Cup records. Finally, all of the records highlighted herein, that were either set or tied by teams and individuals, still stand as of this book's publication date.

* FIFA stands for Fédération Internationale de Football Association, whose full name in English is translated as "International Federation of Association Football." FIFA is the global governing organization for both men's and women's soccer.

The FIFA World Cup

Every four years, soccer fans around the globe are fired up —
To watch the world's most popular sporting event, the FIFA World Cup!

Qualifying for the World Cup tournament is every nation's plan.
In the year 1930, in the South American country of Uruguay, is when and where it all began.

Only eight countries have ever won the men's World Cup, and six of these nations won as a host.
Brazil's 229 goals, 73 wins, 21 tournament appearances, and 5 championships are the most.
In the 1958 World Cup, Brazil's performances in Sweden were great:
Brazil remains the only non-European nation to have won a men's World Cup in Europe, which it did in 1958.

Defensemen Hilderaldo Luiz Bellini (the captain in 1958), Djalma Pereira Dias dos Santos, and Nílton dos Santos, midfielder José Ely de Miranda, better known as "Zito," and midfielder Waldyr "Didi" Pereira came through,

Along with striker Edvaldo Jizídio "Vavá" Neto and right winger Manuel Francisco dos Santos, better known as "Garrincha," in 1958 and 1962.

By scoring four goals to help Brazil win the 1962 World Cup in Chile, Garrincha deserved a big "thank you,"

So he won the Golden Boot (for the top goal scorer of the tournament) and the Golden Ball (for the best player of the tournament) awards in 1962.

With captain/defenseman Carlos Alberto "Capita" Torres and midfielder Gérson de Oliveira Nunes, the Brazilians continued to glow;

Midfielder Roberto Rivellino and right winger Jair Ventura "Jairzinho" Filho also helped them win the 1970 World Cup in Mexico.

In 1958, 1962, and 1970, forward/midfielder Edson Arantes do Nascimento, better known as "Pelé," demonstrated his winning will:

He became the first and only soccer player to help his team win three World Cups — for the South American country of Brazil!

In 1958, 1962, and 1970, Mário Jorge Lobo Zagallo helped Brazil win the World Cup thrice,

As Brazil's manager (head coach) once, in 1970, and as an offensive player twice.

In 1994, defenseman Márcio Roberto dos Santos and defender Jorge de Amorim Campos, better known as "Jorginho," were terrific teammates;

Along with captain/midfielder Carlos Caetano Bledorn Verri, better known as "Dunga," and striker Romário de Souza Faria, they led Brazil to the 1994 World Cup title in the United States.

Defenseman Roberto Carlos da Silva Rocha, midfielder Rivaldo Vítor Barbosa Ferreira, and striker Ronaldo Luís Nazário de Lima implemented an effective plan;

So, along with midfielder Ronaldo de Assis Moreira, better known as "Ronaldinho," they led Brazil to the 2002 World Cup championship in South Korea and Japan.

From 1998 through 2006, the Brazilian national team featured some of the best soccer performances ever seen;

Over those three tournaments, the team's star striker, Ronaldo, scored the second-most goals in the history of the men's World Cup, with a total of 15.

For Brazilians, watching World Cup soccer was a thrill,

Because seven Final appearances were earned by Brazil.

With four World Cup championships, Italy scored goals and stopped opposing offenses from scoring at a very fast rate;

The Italian national team became the first country to win two consecutive World Cups, powered by midfielder/forward Giovanni Ferrari, forward Giuseppe "Peppino" Meazza (the captain in 1938), and defenseman Eraldo Monzeglio, in 1934 and 1938.

In 1934 and 1938, Italy's Vittorio Pozzo gave great advice,

Becoming the first manager to win the World Cup twice.

Midfielders Attilio Ferraris and Luis Felipe Monti and strikers Enrique Guaita and Angelo Schiavio had a great rapport

With forward/winger Raimundo Bibiani "Mumo" Orsi, helping host Italy win the World Cup in 1934.

When Italy won its second consecutive World Cup, which was hosted in France, defensemen Alfredo Foni and Pietro Rava worked very well together; so it was soccer fate

When midfielder Miguel Ángel Andreolo Frodella, better known as Michele Andreolo, midfielder Ugo Locatelli, striker Luigi Colausig, better known as "Gino Colaussi," and striker Silvio Gioacchino Italo Piola also led Italy to the World Cup title in 1938.

The Italians also implemented their bag of tricks

When they won two more World Cups in 1982 and 2006.

On 7/11/82, due to Italy's defensemen Fulvio Collovati and Claudio Gentile, West Germany's offensive efforts resulted in little gain;

At the age of 40 years and 133 days, captain and goalie Dino Zoff became the oldest player to appear in a World Cup Final and also the oldest World Cup champion, when Italy beat West Germany 3-1 in Madrid, Spain.

In the 1982 World Cup, striker Paolo Rossi scored six goals, so he knew how to effectively shoot;

For his offensive prowess, Paolo Rossi won two terrific tournament awards: the Golden Ball and the Golden Boot.

On 7/9/06, when the World Cup Final was held in Germany, despite a game tied 1-1 after overtime, the Italian players didn't have a single doubt:

At Olympiastadion Berlin, they beat France when all five of their kickers scored in a 5-3 penalty shootout.

Goalie Gianluigi "Gigi" Buffon, defensemen Fabio Cannavaro (captain) and Gianluca Zambrotta, midfielders Gennaro Ivan "Rino" Gattuso and Andrea Pirlo, striker Luca Toni, and attacking midfielder Francesco Totti led Italy to its fourth World Cup championship in 2006.

More soccer history: In the United States of America, in the inaugural 2001-2002 Major Indoor Soccer League (MISL) season and also in the 2006-2007 MISL season, the Major Indoor Soccer League champion was the Philadelphia KiXX.

The men's soccer teams that represented West Germany and later a reunified Germany would soar:
They scored 226 tournament goals, and their number of World Cup championships reached four.
With a record eight World Cup Final appearances, German soccer has lore;
The German national team has also placed a record thirteen times in the "Final Four."
In the 1954 World Cup Final at Bern, Switzerland's Wankdorf Stadium, due to the one goal by forward Maximilian Morlock and the two goals that forward Helmut Rahn would score,
West Germany defeated Hungary by the score of 3-2 in "The Miracle of Bern" on July 4, 1954.
Attacking midfielder Friedrich "Fritz" Walter, the captain of the 1954 squad, and striker Ottmar Kurt Herrmann Walter were like no others:
They were the first World Cup champions to play on the same team who were brothers.
In the 1974 World Cup Final at Munich, Germany's Olympiastadion, for West Germany's Gerhard "Gerd" Müller's Cup-clinching goal and for the efforts of attacking midfielder Wolfgang Overath, German fans gave a loud roar;
They also cheered for goalie Josef Dieter "Sepp" Maier, defensemen Paul Breitner and Hans-Hubert "Berti" Vogts, and captain/defender Franz Anton Beckenbauer during West Germany's 2-1 win over the Netherlands on July 7, 1974.
On 7/8/90, in the World Cup Final at Rome, Italy's Stadio Olimpico, during a 1-0 contest between West Germany and Argentina, defender Andreas "Andy" Brehme scored the Cup-clinching goal on a penalty kick, so there was great cause for celebration and certainly no cause for reproach.
In addition, West Germany's 1990 World Cup championship team featured such standouts as captain/ midfielder Lothar Herbert Matthäus, striker Jürgen Klinsmann, and Franz Beckenbauer, who was now the team's head coach.
From 1982 through 1998, Lothar Matthäus set a men's World Cup record by playing in 25 games, so he would impress.
From 2002 through 2014, with his men's World Cup record of 16 goals, German striker Miroslav Josef Klose was also a success.
On 7/8/14, in Germany's 7-1 win over host Brazil, midfielder Toni Kroos scored two goals 69 seconds apart, the quickest time for the same player to score twice in a men's World Cup game; in just 29 minutes, Germany scored the five fastest goals to begin a men's World Cup contest; and the Germans also set two World Cup records for a semifinal match by scoring seven (consecutive) goals and winning by the margin of six goals — Germany was a scoring machine!
Five days later, in Germany's 1-0 win over Argentina, substitute Mario Götze scored an overtime Cup-clinching goal, becoming the first and only sub to score the game-winning goal in a World Cup Final — and Germany became the first European nation to win a men's World Cup in the Americas, in 2014.

In the 2014 World Cup, Manager Joachim Löw and goalie Manuel Peter Neuer were held in high esteem;
Along with defenseman Mats Julian Hummels and forward Thomas Müller, all were marvelous members of Germany's World Cup championship team.

In the men's World Cup, West Germany's/Germany's Jürgen Klinsmann (1990-1998), Brazil's Ronaldo (1998-2006), and Germany's Miroslav Klose (2002-2010) are the only three players to each have three different tournaments of scoring at least three goals;
The stellar scoring efforts of these three soccer stars stranded their opponents in the shoals.
Ronaldo (1998-2006) and Klose (2002-2014) are the only two players in men's World Cup history to have scored at least one goal in 11 different matches;
These soccer contests also featured some amazing assists, superb saves, and spectacular catches.

For one particular South American country, the 1930 and 1950 World Cups were both very nice;
Forwards José Pedro Cea and Óscar Omar Míguez Antón, respectively, each scored five goals, so Uruguay won the World Cup twice.
In 1930, captain/defenseman José Nasazzi Yarra and midfielders José Leandro Andrade and Álvaro Antonio Gestido Pose hustled from goalpost to goalpost;
Uruguay also featured goalie Enrique Pedro Ballestrero Griffo and forwards Héctor Castro and Héctor Pedro Scarone Beretta, as the inaugural World Cup was won by the host.
When Uruguay won the 1950 World Cup in Brazil, the efforts of goalkeeper Roque Gastón Máspoli Arbelvide and midfielder Víctor Pablo Rodríguez Andrade were very nifty;
The same could be said of right winger Alcides Edgardo Ghiggia Pereyra, captain/midfielder Obdulio Jacinto Muiños Varela, and forward Juan Alberto "Pepe" Schiaffino Villano in 1950.

Although France's national team did not ultimately prevail in the 1958 World Cup, French fans attending that series of matches in Sweden were still given many reasons to dance:
Star striker Just Louis Fontaine set two World Cup records for a single tournament with his 13 goals and six consecutive games of scoring at least one goal (matched by Brazil's Jairzinho in 1970) while playing for France.

To be historically accurate and precise,
The South American country of Argentina won the World Cup twice.
For host Argentina, goalkeeper Ubaldo Matildo Fillol and captain/defender Daniel Alberto Passarella would dominate,
Along with defenseman Alberto César Tarantini, when Argentina won the World Cup in 1978.
Also in 1978, for scoring six goals, striker Mario Alberto Kempes Chiodi was adored,
So he won both the Golden Ball Award and the Golden Boot Award.
In each World Cup contest in 1986, captain/midfielder Diego Armando Maradona Franco put on a super show:
He scored five goals over seven games in the stadiums of Puebla and Mexico City in Mexico.
On 6/22/86, in a quarterfinal contest against England, Diego Maradona found the open holes
For his "Hand of God" and "Goal of the Century" goals!
The soccer heroics of Diego Maradona would enthrall,
So his team won the 1986 World Cup, and he won the Golden Ball.

England's 1966 squad and France's 1998 team both represented national aspirations;
So, to the delight of their fans, they won World Cup tournaments as host nations.
Defensemen George Reginald Cohen and Robert Frederick Chelsea "Bobby" Moore (captain) led the English front,
Along with midfielder Robert "Bobby" Charlton, Bobby's brother/defenseman John "Jack" Charlton, goalie Gordon Banks, and forward Roger Hunt.
On 7/30/66, English striker Geoffrey Charles "Geoff" Hurst was very quick;
Against West Germany, he recorded the first and only men's World Cup Final hat trick!
On 7/12/98, in the World Cup Final between France and Brazil, the French players, like defensemen Marcel Desailly (born Odenke Abbey) and Ruddy Lilian Thuram-Ulien, knew their roles,
Along with goalie Fabien Alain Barthez and captain/midfielder Didier Claude Deschamps; so did France's midfielder Zinedine Yazid Zidane, who scored two goals.

Brazil's Vavá (1958 and 1962), Brazil's Pelé (1958 and 1970), West Germany's Paul Breitner (1974 and 1982), and France's Zinedine Zidane (1998 and 2006) had soccer careers that were filled with ups and downs, but more ups.
They are the only four players to ever score in two World Cup Final matches, so they each excelled in two different World Cups.

Had Brazil's Vavá (1958 and 1962), England's Geoff Hurst (1966), Brazil's Pelé (1958 and 1970), and France's Zinedine Zidane (1998 and 2006) run for president or prime minister in their respective country's elections, they would have been popular selections at the polls,
Because in the entire history of men's World Cup Final matches, stretching back almost a century now, these are the only four players to ever score a total of three goals.

At the 2010 World Cup in South Africa, soccer fans played plastic horns called vuvuzelas, sometimes to distract the opponents and sometimes just to entertain;
On 7/11/10, in the World Cup Final between Spain and the Netherlands, a 1-0 contest, an overtime goal by midfielder Andrés Iniesta Luján clinched the World Cup for Spain.
During this tournament, Manager Vicente del Bosque González and defensemen Sergio Ramos García and Carles Puyol Saforcada put forth their best efforts for Spain in each game,
Along with captain/goalkeeper Iker Casillas Fernández, striker David Villa Sánchez, and "Xavi," which was midfielder Xavier Hernández Creus' nickname.

Now at Fisht Olympic Stadium in Sochi, Russia, on June 15, 2018, Portugal's Cristiano Ronaldo dos Santos Aveiro made many marvelous plays;
In a 3-3 draw between Portugal and Spain, he became the oldest player in a men's World Cup contest to record a hat trick, at the age of 33 years and 130 days.

West Germany's Uwe Seeler (1958-1970), Brazil's Pelé (1958-1970), Germany's Miroslav Klose (2002-2014), and Portugal's Cristiano Ronaldo (2006-2018) all had a gift for finding the open hole,
So they share the men's World Cup record for the most tournaments — four each — with at least one goal.

On 6/25/18, at Russia's Volgograd Arena, in a match between Egypt and Saudi Arabia, Egypt's goalkeeper, Essam Kamal Tawfiq El Hadary, deserved much praise
When he set three World Cup records — the oldest player to debut in a World Cup game, the oldest player to play in a World Cup contest, and the oldest captain of a team in a World Cup match — at the incredible age of 45 years and 161 days.

In 2018, England's World Cup contests were watched by English guitarist Eric Patrick Clapton.
During the 2018 World Cup, Mexico's Rafael Márquez Álvarez set two World Cup career records with his fifth tournament and 17th match as a team captain.

Mexico's Antonio Félix Carbajal Rodríguez (1950-1966), West Germany's/Germany's Lothar Matthäus (1982-1998), and Mexico's Rafael Márquez (2002-2018) all demonstrated longevity and drive;
As a result, they share the men's World Cup record for the greatest number of tournament appearances: five.

On 7/15/18, in the World Cup Final at Moscow, Russia's Luzhniki Stadium, playing against France, Croatia didn't stand a chance.
Due to the efforts of head coach Didier Deschamps, forwards Antoine Griezmann and Kylian Mbappé Lottin, and defenseman Raphaël Xavier Varane, a second World Cup championship was claimed by France.
Over World Cup history, Brazil's Mário Zagallo (a player in 1958 and 1962, and then the head coach in 1970), West Germany's Franz Beckenbauer (a player in 1974, and then the head coach in 1990), and France's Didier Deschamps (a player in 1998, and then the head coach in 2018) each implemented an amazing approach;
They each helped their respective country win World Cups, both as a player *and* as a head coach.
On the world's biggest stage, Brazil's Pelé, at the age of 17, and France's Kylian Mbappé, at the age of 19, showed at a young age that their soccer intelligence was already keen:
In the World Cup Final of 1958 and in the World Cup Final of 2018, they each, respectively, scored at least one goal — as a teen!

In the history of the FIFA World Cup, on their home continent, European teams have been royal:
They have won 10 out of their 12 World Cup championships on their own soil.
South American squads have won the other nine times.
I hope you enjoyed reading these FIFA World Cup rhymes!

Pelé

Watching forward/midfielder Edson Arantes do Nascimento score goals with either foot was a soccer thrill.

On October 23, 1940, he was born in Três Corações, a city in the South American country of Brazil.

His given name was intended to honor inventor Thomas Alva Edison, but during his school days, "Pelé became

His eternal nickname, the appellation under which he achieved his global fame.

Pelé's reflexes were very quick.

He popularized the "bicycle kick."

I'm sure that to the seasoned sports fan, it will come as no shocker

That Pelé's father, João Ramos do Nascimento, nicknamed "Dondinho," was a professional in soccer.

When evaluating soccer players in Brazil, scout Waldemar de Brito, a former Brazilian forward, told the truth;
Waldemar also predicted that Pelé would become the greatest soccer player ever, after discovering him in his youth.

On 9/7/56, at the youthful age of fifteen, for the Santos Futebol Clube, Pelé came through:
As his team beat the Corinthians Futebol Clube de Santo André 7-1, he scored a goal in his professional debut!

On 7/7/57, in his first international match for Brazil, at the age of 16 years and 259 days, Pelé knew his role;
Against visiting victorious Argentina, he became the youngest soccer player for Brazil to ever score an international goal.

In 1957, while scoring 17 goals for Santos in the Brazilian state of São Paulo, Pelé didn't display any fatigue;
He began a record-setting nine-year streak as the leading goal scorer in the Campeonato Paulista Série A1, São Paulo's top soccer league.

On 6/19/58, at Ullevi, a large stadium in Gothenburg, Sweden, while playing for the Brazilian national team at the age of 17 years and 239 days, Pelé would soar:
In a FIFA World Cup quarterfinal match against Wales, he scored the only goal of the contest and became the youngest player in a men's World Cup contest to ever score!

On 6/24/58, in Brazil's World Cup semifinal victory over France, at the age of 17 years and 244 days, Pelé was very quick:
In the Stockholm suburb of Solna at Råsunda Stadium, he scored three goals, becoming the youngest player to ever record a World Cup hat trick!

On 6/29/58, again at Råsunda Stadium, in the World Cup Final, when Brazil beat host Sweden by the score of 5-2, at the age of 17 years and 249 days, Pelé found the open holes;
Pelé became the youngest participant in a World Cup Final, the youngest player to score a goal in a World Cup Final, and the youngest World Cup champion — he scored two goals!

In the 1958 World Cup, Pelé scored six goals for Brazil and won the Best Young Player Award of the tournament, so he stood tall;
Pelé was also named a World Cup All-Star, and since he was named the second best player of the tournament, he won the Silver Ball.

Pelé set a Campeonato Paulista Série A1 single-season record with his 58 goals, so his scoring prowess was great;
In the first of ten times, Pelé led Santos to the Campeonato Paulista Série A1 title, and for Santos and Brazil, he scored a combined 75 goals in 1958.

From 3/7/59 through 4/4/59, in the South American Football Championship, Brazil's Pelé didn't boast:
Even though host Argentina won the championship, he was named the best player of the tournament, and his eight goals were the most.

In an annual Brazilian tournament between the Rio de Janeiro and São Paulo teams called the Torneio Rio-São Paulo, Pelé's performances were fine;
In the first of four times (including 1963 when Pele was the leading goal scorer), he helped Santos, his São Paulo club, win this tournament in 1959.

Pelé's career-high 127 goals in 1959 marked another amazing year in his soccer career.
Surely, sports fans around the world who witnessed this feat gave him a loud cheer.

In 1961, in the Taca Brasil (Brazil's annual soccer championship), Pelé's team, Santos, hustled a ton;
In the first of five consecutive times, due to Pelé's terrific Taca Brasil performances, his club won.

On 5/30/62, in Brazil's World Cup opener against Mexico, the Brazilian team would persist;
At Estadio Sausalito in Viña del Mar, Chile, in Brazil's 2-0 win, Pelé scored a goal and earned an assist.

In the 1962 World Cup, which was held in the South American country of Chile, Brazil had a lot of fun;
Even though Pelé got injured in Brazil's second game of the tournament — at the age of 21 — he became the youngest two-time World Cup champion when his team won.

In 1962 and 1963, when South American teams faced each other, and when South American clubs competed against European teams, Pelé was all fired up:
He led Santos to victories in, respectively, the Copa Libertadores (Libertadores Cup) and the Intercontinental Cup.
In both Intercontinental Cups, Pelé was the top goal scorer,
Which was exciting, just like a journey for an explorer.
In both of these tournaments, Brazil reached soccer heaven;
Pelé's number of goals set the Intercontinental Cup career record — seven.

On 11/21/64, as host Santos shut out the Botafogo Futebol Clube 11-0, Pelé impressed;
For a single professional soccer game, he scored eight goals, which was his career best!

While playing for Santos, Pelé became a big part of soccer lore:
He was the top goal scorer in the Taca Brasil in 1961, 1963, and 1964.

For Santos, Pelé demonstrated much offensive drive:
He led the Copa Libertadores with eight goals in 1965.

On 7/12/66, in a World Cup match in England that featured only two goals, Pelé effectively covered his area;
He and right winger Manuel Francisco dos Santos, better known as "Garrincha," each scored a goal when Brazil shut out Bulgaria.

Playing 40 games together for their country of Brazil, the tandem of Pelé and Garrincha was quite a catch;
Since Brazil's record was 36-0-4, when opposing defenders tried to cover this dynamic duo in a match, it was always a *mis*match.

From 8/24/68 through 12/10/68, Santos won the Torneio Roberto Gomes Pedrosa championship, which was for Brazil's soccer title, so Pelé's squad made many superb kicks.
Since Pelé had already helped Santos win five Taca Brasil titles, the number of Brazilian championships that he helped his club win reached six.

On 11/19/69, as visiting Santos beat the Club de Regatas Vasco da Gama, with the right foot that he favored for penalty kicks (and free kicks), Pelé showed his precise control;
In the second half of a 2-1 contest at Rio de Janeiro's Estádio Jornalista Mário Filho (nicknamed "Maracanã"), he scored the game-winning goal on a penalty kick — his 1,000th career goal!
As a result of his stunning soccer display,
November 19th came to be celebrated in Santos as Pelé Day.

For Santos, the league champions, Pelé's offensive skills were divine:
He led the Campeonato Paulista Série A1 with 26 goals in 1969.

In the 1970 World Cup, while playing for the Brazilian national team, Pelé made the Czechoslovakian and Romanian teams pay:
At Guadalajara, Mexico's Jalisco Stadium, he scored a combined three goals — including two game-winners — against these two European teams, so Brazil beat both of them in group play.

West Germany's Uwe Seeler (1958-1970), Brazil's Pelé (1958-1970), Germany's Miroslav Josef Klose (2002-2014), and Portugal's Cristiano Ronaldo dos Santos Aveiro (2006-2018) each were superstars in their respective lineups;
In the entire history of the FIFA World Cup, which dates back to 1930, they are the only four players to ever score a goal in four men's World Cups.

On 6/21/70, at Mexico City's Azteca Stadium, in the World Cup Final, with his two assists, Pelé earned his daily bread;
When Brazil beat Italy 4-1, he also scored the first goal of the contest — which was Brazil's 100th World Cup goal — by using his head.

With his Brazilian teammates in the 1958 World Cup Final and also in the 1970 World Cup Final, Pelé had a great rapport.
Pelé became the second of four players to score in the World Cup Final of two different World Cup tournaments, and of players who scored a total of three goals in all matches of the men's World Cup Final, he became the third of four.

In the 1970 World Cup, Pelé was named a tournament All-Star, and he set a World Cup record for a single tournament with his six assists, so his skills continued to enthrall.
Pelé scored four goals and was named the best player of the tournament, so he was awarded the Golden Ball.
In international contests, Pelé's performances made Brazilian soccer a sporting paradise:
He became the first and only soccer player ever to help his team win the World Cup thrice!

In 1970, for helping Brazil's national team win its third World Cup in soccer, Pelé deserved a loud cheer;
He was named the British Broadcasting Corporation (BBC) Overseas Sports Personality of the Year.

On 7/11/71, in his 91st and penultimate international match for the Brazilian national team, Pelé masterfully played his role:
In a 1-1 exhibition draw between host Brazil and Austria, he set a men's soccer record for Brazil by scoring his 77th career international goal.

In 1973, Pelé's 11 goals made him the top goal scorer in the Campeonato Paulista Série A1 for a record 11th season, reaffirming his status as a star to revere.
Santos and the Associacão Portuguesa de Desportos shared the league title, and Pelé was named the South American Footballer of the Year.

On 6/15/75, for a North American Soccer League (NASL) contest between the host New York Cosmos and the Dallas Tornado, ten million television viewers had a fabulous view;
At New York City's Downing Stadium, Pelé earned an assist and scored a goal during a 2-2 tie in his New York Cosmos debut.
There were many people in New York and on TV who saw Pelé's superb skills and his gentlemanly behavior;
So on 6/23/75, he appeared on *Sports Illustrated*'s cover with the caption "PELÉ'S TRIUMPHANT DEBUT: U.S. Soccer Finds a Savior."

In 1976, for the New York Cosmos, Pelé's 13 goals and NASL-leading 18 assists were key,
So he was named the North American Soccer League Most Valuable Player (MVP).

From 1975 through 1977, Americans stayed enthusiastic about soccer because Pelé continued to intrigue;
In those three consecutive years, he was named a first-team All-Star of the North American Soccer League.

In 1977, Pelé's offensive performances were vital,
So his Cosmos won the North American Soccer League title.

Pelé was an ambassador for soccer, and he wanted people around the planet to have great aspirations.
On 9/27/77, in New York City, Pelé received an award for his support of the United Nations Children's
Fund and a certificate stating that he was "A Citizen of the World," from the United Nations.

On 10/1/77, in an exhibition match at Giants Stadium in northern New Jersey, Pelé participated in his
final soccer game.
Playing for the Cosmos in the first half, he scored the game-tying goal with his awesome aim.
For the Cosmos, Pelé hustled time and again.
In a halftime ceremony, they retired his uniform number 10.
On this day, Pelé lived a one-of-a-kind soccer dream;
In the second half of the match, he played for Santos, his original team.
After this historic one-of-a-kind contest, which ended in a Cosmos' 2-1 victory, Pelé finally retired.
Pelé's 1,283 goals in his professional career (*1283* became his 2012 book title) are still much admired!

Pelé continued to support children and spread goodwill across the globe, from country to country and
state to state;
So, back in New York City, he won the Planetary Citizens' inaugural International Peace Award on
May 18, 1978.

In 1981, Pelé appeared with actor Maurice Joseph Micklewhite Jr. (Michael Caine), actor Michael
Sylvester Gardenzio **Stallone**, and several actual soccer stars in a sports World War II movie.
Playing for a soccer team of Allied prisoners of war, Pelé scored the game-tying goal with a bicycle
kick, so his club tied Germany's national soccer team 4-4; with such an intriguing cast, *Escape to
Victory* was groovy.

Though originally from Brazil, Pelé was someone that the entire world was fortunate enough to
inherit;
So in 1984, for a lifetime of contributions to soccer, he was awarded the FIFA Order of Merit.

Famous for caring about people, the Earth's environment, and the animals on our planet, Pelé deserved
a big "thank you,"
So he was named a United Nations ambassador for ecology and the environment in 1992.

Named a goodwill ambassador by the United Nations in April 1994, there was much humanitarian support
Provided by Pelé when he became a United Nations Educational, Scientific and Cultural Organization (UNESCO) Champion for Sport.

In 1997, the English soccer players were very good.
That same year, Pelé received an honorary British knighthood.

Benefiting Brazilian soccer players, leagues, and organizations was Pelé's chosen fate
When he served as Brazil's Extraordinary Minister for Sport from 1995 to 1998.
In 1998, the newly created Pelé Law made sure that teams would adhere to business laws and pay taxes within two years.
This law also allowed clubs to create their own leagues, so Pelé's efforts to improve Brazilian soccer deserved many cheers.

During his professional soccer career, Pelé set records with his 92 hat tricks and 470 Campeonato Paulista Série A1 goals, so he scored at a rapid rate.
As a forward, like Argentina's Diego Armando Maradona Franco, Pelé was named to the World Team of the 20th Century in 1998.

For a ceremony at the Meadowlands Sports Complex, Pelé was genuine
When he was inducted into the Sports Hall of Fame of New Jersey on May 13, 1999.

For 20th century honors, Pelé was named the Athlete of the Century by the International Olympic Committee (IOC), the Reuters Sports Personality of the Century, *France Football*'s Football Player of the Century, and *World Soccer*'s Greatest Football Player of the Century, so his reputation continued to impress.
Pelé was also named the World Player of the Century, South America's Player of the Century, and Brazil's Player of the Century by the International Federation of Football History & Statistics (IFFHS).

On 5/25/00, in Monte Carlo, Monaco, the legendary former president of South Africa gave a superb speech which recognized that this soccer legend was a fabulous fella;
Pelé won the inaugural Laureus Lifetime Achievement Award for his soccer career that inspired folks around the world — and Pelé's presenter was none other than Nelson Rolihlahla Mandela!

On 12/11/00, for a 20th century honor, Brazil's Pelé and Argentina's Diego Maradona were adored:
FIFA announced them as the co-winners of the FIFA Player of the Century Award!

Because of their contributions to soccer, World Cup champions Pelé and West Germany's Franz Anton Beckenbauer would soar,
So at the FIFA headquarters in Zürich, Switzerland, they each received the award for the FIFA Centennial Order of Merit, on September 23, 2004.

On 12/11/05, at London, England's BBC Television Centre, Pelé was full of glee
When he received the Sports Personality of the Year Lifetime Achievement Award from the BBC.

In 2006, as a global icon and a world traveler, Pelé knew his geography.
That same year, he finally published the long-awaited *Pele: The Autobiography*.

In February 2011, from a historical point of view,
Pelé was named one of The 25 Coolest Athletes of All Time by the magazine *GQ*.

In 2012, Pelé received two awards, the Children in Need Award from UNESCO for helping kids, and the Golden Foot Award, an honor chosen by the media and the public, for being the greatest soccer player of all time.
That same year, outfielder Michael Nelson "Mike" Trout, nicknamed "The Millville Meteor," won the American League Rookie of the Year Award when he played for the Los Angeles Angels of Anaheim.

A panel of soccer experts proclaimed Pelé's performances to be amazing and his soccer intelligence keen,
So as a forward, he was named as one of the Greatest XI of All Time by *World Soccer* magazine in July 2013.

At Switzerland's Zürich Convention Center for a spectacular soccer ceremony, Pelé was again seen
When he received an honorary FIFA Ballon d'Or Award for his superb career on January 13, 2014.

In 2014, the Pelé Museum opened in Santos, so fans learned more about the brightest star from soccer's golden age.
That same year, Pelé published *Why Soccer Matters*, a history of the sport on the international stage.

On 6/16/16, at his museum to receive the International Olympic Committee's greatest honor, Pelé would collect

An IOC Olympic Order that recognized him for displaying the Olympic values of friendship, excellence, and respect.

When Pelé set a Santos record with his 643 goals, he worked very well with his teammates and demonstrated much dedication.

On 1/21/18, Pelé was recognized as the winner of the FWA Tribute Award from the Football Writers' Association.

Also, on 9/13/18, with the aim of helping children educationally and reducing child poverty, he announced a new charity, the Pelé Foundation.

Pelé famously proclaimed that soccer was "The Beautiful Game."

Over time, he was inducted into the Brazilian Football Museum, Goal, International Football, Long Island Soccer Player, National Soccer, World Soccer, and World Sports Humanitarian Halls of Fame.

During Pelé's soccer career, "The King of Football" and "The King" were also his nicknames.

In Maceió, Brazil, Estádio Rei Pelé (King Pelé Stadium) is mainly used for soccer games.

Success had filled Pelé's legendary career to the brim,

So the town of Três Corações, where he was born, now features a statue of him.

In this Brazilian city, you should also visit the Edson Arantes do Nascimento Street.

Due to Pelé's incredible international performances, Brazil's soccer team was elite.

Watching Pelé set a record for Brazil with his seven hat tricks, as well as score 12 goals for his country over four World Cups, was a pleasure.

His offensive skills were so outstanding that in 1961 the national government even passed a law proclaiming Pelé an official Brazilian treasure.

In addition, Brazil honored his 1,000th career goal with a 1969 postage stamp.

What an achievement for a soccer player: Pelé became the only three-time World Cup champ!

Defenders and goalies just couldn't stop Pelé in his prime:

That's why he is the greatest soccer player of all time!

Where Basketball Meets Soccer

Basketball and soccer are two of the world's most popular sports. Helmets aren't worn, nor even hats, but players wear shirts and shorts.

You can work on your ball control or you can practice scoring in basketball and soccer whether you are alone or with your terrific teammates.

Ironically, basketball was invented in 1891 by a *Canadian*, physical education teacher James Naismith, who wanted to help track & field athletes stay in shape in the wintertime in Springfield, Massachusetts, in the northeastern United States.

Soccer had its rules drafted in London, England, in 1863 by Ebenezer Cobb Morley and agreed on by the various schools and soccer clubs who were members of a newly established governing group, The Football Association.

This effort to standardize the game allowed the sport to grow internationally over the following decades because near-identical sets of rules would come to be administered by each country's own soccer governance organization.

Basketball is played on a court;
Give your teammates support!
Soccer is played on a field;
Don't ever yield!

Basketball and soccer share several similarities;
Yes, they've got things in common, not just disparities.
For example, both sports are played with a good-sized round ball — in fact, basketball was originally played with a *soccer ball*:
Despite what you might think, another commonality would be that a player can be relatively small or toweringly tall.
The dimensions of the playing areas are rectangular,
Not circular or triangular.
That both sports focus on feet is no mere quirk,
Because both games demand fantastic footwork.
Players can dribble or pass the ball;
Upon their ball control, sporting fortunes rise or fall.
After each score, the crowd will roar,
As players try to paint themselves into sporting lore.
In both mind and body, a winner is fit;
A real competitor will never quit.
Basketball and soccer can both be played almost anywhere.
A professional in either of these two sports can become a millionaire.

There is one man singularly situated to demonstrate this basketball-soccer solidarity,
A man who played basketball professionally, but has set up annual soccer games for charity.
That altruistic athlete, Stephen John "Steve" Nash — whose father was a semi-professional soccer player — was just as popular as any mayor,
Because while growing up in Canada, Steve was a both a superb basketball and soccer player.
For his stellar 18-year National Basketball Association (NBA) career, guard Steve Nash deserved much acclaim,
So on September 7, 2018, he was inducted into the Naismith Memorial Basketball Hall of Fame.
His Steve Nash Foundation helps underserved kids in America and Canada by staging charity soccer games in New York City and Los Angeles, each coast's city of greatest renown;
You can register to play in a Charity Shield soccer game, or you can watch NBA and pro soccer stars compete in the charity soccer game known as the Showdown.

Around the world, both sports continue to enthrall.
Good people, always remember: Never argue with an official's call —
So you can stay focused on having a good time playing soccer and basketball!

Diego Maradona

In the world of soccer, especially in South America, Diego Armando Maradona Franco will always be divine.
Born on October 30, 1960, in Lanús, Argentina, near the country's capital of Buenos Aires, he was an ardent Argentine!
"The Golden Boy" became
His gilded nickname.

Left-footed midfielder Diego Maradona was a prodigy whose road to soccer stardom took an early route;
In March 1969, at the age of eight, he was identified by Francisco Cornejo, an Asociación Atlética Argentinos Juniors scout.

For the Argentinos Juniors, Diego Maradona began his lifelong soccer dream
With the Cebollitas (Little Onions), the franchise's junior team.

On 10/20/76, in Buenos Aires, Argentina, soccer fans had a fabulous view
When, at the age of 15, for the host Argentinos Juniors, Maradona made his professional debut.

Even as a teenager, Diego Maradona scored many goals and earned many assists, and working hard
became his theme.
On 2/27/77, in host Argentina's 5-1 victory over Hungary, he debuted for Argentina's national team.

The Argentinos Juniors' Diego Maradona and the Quilmes Atlético Club's Luis Antonio Andreuchi
each scored 22 goals, which led Argentina's Campeonato Metropolitano (Metropolitan Championship)
in 1978.
At the youthful age of seventeen, Diego Maradona became the youngest leading goal scorer in
Argentina's Primera División (First Division), so his performances were great.

On 6/2/79, when Argentina beat host Scotland 3-1, Diego knew his role;
At only eighteen years old, he scored his first international goal.

From 8/26/79 through 9/7/79, in the FIFA World Youth Championship, Diego scored five goals in
Japan, so fans obviously weren't bored;
His team, Argentina, won the championship, and Maradona was named the best player of the
tournament, so he won the Golden Ball Award.

In 1979, while playing for the Argentinos Juniors, Diego Maradona was a star to revere:
In the first of two consecutive years, he was named the South American Footballer of the Year.

From 1979 through 1981, while playing two seasons for the Argentinos Juniors and then one season
for the Club Atlético Boca Juniors, Diego scored goals at a fast clip;
In those three consecutive years, Maradona was named Argentina's Footballer of the Year, and in 1979
and 1980, he was the top goal scorer in two Argentine championships: the Metropolitan Championship
and the Campeonato Nacional (National Championship).

In Argentina, Diego Maradona hustled a ton,
As he helped the Boca Juniors win the Metropolitan Championship in 1981.

On 6/18/82, in a FIFA World Cup contest in Alicante, Spain, when Argentina defeated Hungary 4-1, Diego continued to impress:
Maradona scored two goals that day, including the game-winning goal, as he continued his sensational soccer success.

On 6/29/82, when Argentina faced Italy in a second-round match, Argentine fans had the right to make scowls,
Because at Barcelona, Spain's Sarrià Stadium, Diego Maradona set a World Cup single-game record by suffering 23 fouls.

In 1982-1983, again playing soccer in Spain, Diego Maradona was extremely fired up,
As he greatly helped the Futbol Club Barcelona win the Copa de la Liga (League Cup), the Copa del Rey (King's Cup), and the Supercopa de España (Spanish Super Cup).

In 1984-1985, when Diego played for the Societá Sportiva Calcio Napoli in Serie A, *Guerin Sportivo* was very wise:
This Italian sports magazine calculated him as the top-rated player in Serie A, so he won its Golden Guerin Prize.
During his first season in Serie A, Maradona led Napoli with 14 goals, leaving his opponents stunned.
In 1985, he was named an ambassador for UNICEF — the organization originally known as the United Nations International Children's Emergency Fund.

On 6/2/86, in Mexico City, when Argentina defeated South Korea 3-1, Diego assisted on all three of Argentina's goals, so he was supreme;
Maradona appeared in the first of 16 matches as a World Cup captain, which would set a record for Argentina, so he lived a soccer dream.

On 6/5/86, when facing Italy in Puebla, Mexico, Argentina continued to rely
On Diego Maradona, who scored a World Cup goal in a 1-1 tie.

On 6/10/86, when facing Bulgaria in Mexico City, Argentina didn't have a single doubt;
In a 2-0 World Cup contest, Diego Maradona had an assist as his team recorded a shutout.

On 6/22/86, in a World Cup quarterfinal contest, Diego found the open holes;
When Argentina defeated England 2-1, he scored two legendary goals.
In Mexico City, Maradona's first goal would enthrall;
It became known as the "Hand of God," yet it was a handball.
Four minutes later, dribbling more than half the field and past five English players, Diego was in control
When he scored what came to be known as his greatest goal!
English goalie Peter Leslie Shilton tried but failed to save the ball with his hands,
His second goal was later voted as the FIFA World Cup Goal of the Century by the fans.
Thus, with his two historic goals, Diego Maradona led the Argentine attack,
Azteca Stadium later memorialized Diego Maradona's two feats, honoring his "Hand of God" goal with a statue and his "Goal of the Century" with a plaque.

On 6/25/86, in a World Cup semifinal contest played at Mexico City's Azteca Stadium, Diego continued to make history;
Maradona scored two goals as his squad shut out Belgium 2-0, so the reason why Argentina won the contest was obviously no mystery.

On 6/29/86, in the World Cup Final at Mexico City's Azteca Stadium, Diego Maradona continued to persist;
Argentina defeated West Germany by the score of 3-2, propelled by his game-winning assist!

In the 1986 World Cup, despite getting fouled 53 times, a record for a single World Cup tournament, Diego Maradona's performances were adored:
Due to Diego's five goals and tournament-leading five assists, he was named the best player of the tournament, thereby winning the Golden Ball Award.
Maradona became the first player to win the Golden Ball Award at both the FIFA World Youth Championship (now renamed the FIFA Under-20 World Cup) and the FIFA World Cup, so he was full of glee.
This feat was later matched, with performances in 2005 and 2014, by a fellow Argentine legend, forward Lionel Andrés Messi Cuccittini, also known as "The Atomic Flea."

Diego Maradona was the best player in the world, so to lead Argentina to the 1986 World Cup title wasn't a shocker.
On 7/7/86, he appeared on the cover of *Sports Illustrated* with a caption emblazoned in all capital letters: "THE KING OF SOCCER."

In 1986, as Diego was named the United Press International Male Athlete of the Year, he was very sincere.

Another honor Maradona earned was that the magazine *World Soccer* named him its World Player of the Year.

Diego Maradona won his second Olimpia Award, given to an Argentine for excellence in sports, because on the soccer field, he implemented his bag of tricks.

For the fourth time, the Circle of Sports Journalists of Buenos Aires named him its Footballer of the Year in 1986.

While playing for Argentina's national soccer team, Diego Maradona stood tall, like a skyscraper.

In addition, he won the Champion of Champions Award in the International category from *L'Équipe*, a French sports newspaper.

Italian fans were in soccer heaven
When Diego helped Napoli win its first-ever Serie A title and also the Coppa Italia (Italian Cup) in 1986-1987.

In 1986 and 1987, Diego Maradona made many marvelous passes and continually scored;
To honor the best soccer player in Europe, the French magazine *Onze* named him the winner of its Onze d'Or Award.

In 1987-1988, when Napoli's Diego Maradona led the Coppa Italia with six goals, he didn't boast.
In addition, his 15 goals in Serie A were the most.

Diego Maradona continued to shine;
He helped Napoli win the Union of European Football Associations (UEFA) Cup in 1988-1989.

In 1989-1990, Diego Maradona put his superb soccer skills on display;
He helped Napoli win the Supercoppa Italiana (Italian Super Cup) and the Serie A.

On 6/24/90, in Italy, a round-of-16 World Cup contest that featured only one goal was a thrill
When Diego Maradona assisted on Claudio Paul Caniggia's game-winning goal against Brazil.

On 7/3/90, in a World Cup semifinal match that was tied 1-1 after overtime, Diego's shot needed to be very quick;
So in a 4-3 penalty shootout, Argentina beat host Italy because he converted the decisive kick!

On 7/8/90, at Rome, Italy's Stadio Olimpico, in another World Cup Final, Argentina faced West Germany again.
In a 1-0 game, due to Andreas "Andy" Brehme's goal on a penalty kick, the West Germans were the victorious men.
But Maradona's team wasn't a disgrace,
Because Argentina earned second place.

Midfielder Diego Maradona was named an All-Star in both the 1986 and 1990 World Cups;
In both of these tournaments, South American and European teams experienced ups, downs, and ups.

For the 1980s, Diego was named Argentina's most important personality in Sports by the Argentine nonprofit Konex Foundation;
So, in 1990, Maradona received the organization's Diamond Konex Award, showing much appreciation.

From 1984-1985 to 1990-1991, Italian fans had a lot to cheer:
Diego scored 115 goals over the course of his Napoli career.

In 1992-1993, Diego Maradona continued to entertain;
He now played for the Sevilla Fútbol Club, a team in the top soccer league of Spain.

On 2/24/93, at Mar del Plata, Argentina's Estadio José María Minella, in a game still tied 1-1 after overtime, Diego Maradona provided an offensive spark;
In a competition between the South American and European champions, he helped Argentina win the Artemio Franchi Trophy by making his penalty kick in a 5-4 shootout, thereby contributing to his team's win over Denmark.

In 1993, Argentine soccer fans felt many joys
When Maradona played for the country's Club Atlético Newell's Old Boys.

On 6/21/94, at Massachusetts' Foxboro Stadium, in Argentina's World Cup opener, Diego would release
A second-half goal as his team scored four goals to shut out Greece.

On 6/25/94, again at Foxboro Stadium, in a 2-1 World Cup game, for his second goal of the contest, Claudio Caniggia kicked the ball, a shot that the goalie couldn't resist;
Claudio Caniggia's game-winning goal against Nigeria was only made possible with Diego Maradona's timely assist.

From 6/13/82 through 6/25/94, Argentina's Diego Maradona used his awesome aim;
Over 21 consecutive World Cup contests, he earned eight career goals and eight assists, while starting in every game.

Temporarily retired as a player and now the manager (head coach), Diego's career continued to thrive, With Argentina's Club Deportivo Mandiyú in 1994 and then with Argentina's Racing Club de Avellaneda in 1995.

Now playing again for the Boca Juniors, Diego demonstrated much drive;
He was named to the South American Team of the Year in 1995.

In 1996, Diego Maradona still stood tall;
For his service to the sport, he received an honorary Golden Ball from the French magazine *France Football*.

From 1995 to 1997, Diego Maradona was held in esteem
As he played for the Boca Juniors, a legendary Argentine team.

Though Diego could still effectively play,
On 10/30/97, he retired on his 37th birthday.

During his professional soccer career, Diego scored 311 club goals, and he recorded assists at a very fast rate.
As a forward, like Brazil's Edson Arantes do Nascimento, better known as "Pelé," Maradona was named to the World Team of the 20th Century in 1998.

On 1/10/99, looking back on Diego Maradona's soccer career, *Marca* was very impressed,
So this Spanish sports newspaper named Diego as the winner of its Marca Leyenda (Marca Legend) Award, because he was one of the best.

For a 20th century Argentine honor, the Circle of Sports Journalists of Buenos Aires named Diego Maradona its Best Athlete of the Century in 1999.
That same year, after *World Soccer* magazine polled its readers, he was named the 2nd Greatest Football Player of the 20th Century, acknowledging his skills were divine.

In Italy, Diego Maradona hustled time and again,
So in 2000, Napoli retired his uniform number 10.
That same year, soccer fans took a look
At *I am the Diego*, his autobiographical book.

In the 20th century, Diego Maradona always enjoyed scoring a goal.
He won the FIFA Player of the Century Award, a fan-based internet poll.
FIFA officials, soccer coaches, and soccer journalists ensured that Pelé wasn't ignored,
So they chose him for this same award.
There was no need to cry,
Because this FIFA honor ended in a tie.
Diego and Pelé were obviously not soccer beginners;
On 12/11/00, for this amazing award, FIFA announced them as the co-winners!

Winning World Cup games for Argentina was the reason Diego Maradona would successfully scheme,
So he received the most votes in a 2002 internet fan poll that named the FIFA World Cup Dream Team.

Of his greatness, international soccer journalists would decree:
So Diego Maradona was honored as a Golden Foot Legend in 2003.

Diego Maradona set an Argentinos Juniors record with his 116 goals, so he filled his early professional career to the brim.
On 12/26/03, the Argentinos Juniors opened their brand-new stadium, Estadio Diego Armando Maradona; in recognition of his achievements, it was named after him.

Throughout his stellar soccer career, Maradona used all of his might.
On 8/15/05, he debuted as the host for his television show: *The 10's Night*.

In 2005 and 2006, Diego was an Argentine resident,
He was also the Boca Juniors' vice president.

Diego Maradona led Argentina to a win in the 1986 World Cup Final, so many Argentine fans celebrated by participating in an impromptu victory parade.
Twenty years later, on 5/27/06, at Old Trafford, a soccer stadium in Manchester, England, he raised money for UNICEF by playing in "Soccer Aid."

On 11/19/08, now the head coach of Argentina's men's soccer team, Diego came through
When his squad defeated host Scotland 1-0, in his national coaching debut.

On 3/22/10, a newspaper based in London, England, would ring its chimes:
Maradona was named the Greatest World Cup Player of All Time by *The Times*.

In the 2010 World Cup, Diego implemented an awesome approach
When he led Argentina's national team to the quarterfinals as its head coach.

When the 1986 World Cup was held in Mexico, Argentina's Diego Maradona used his fabulous frame;
Back in Mexico, on 11/10/11, as a member of its inaugural class, he was inducted into the World Soccer Hall of Fame.

In 2011 and 2012, Diego Maradona knew when to put in a substitute (sub)
When he was the manager of the Al Wasl Football Club, a United Arab Emirates soccer club.

In 2012, to name the winner of the Best Player of the Century, a Globe Soccer Award, there was much cooperation
When Diego Maradona was selected for this honor by the European Association for Football Agents and the European Club Association.

Defensemen had a very difficult time of stopping Diego Maradona when he was in his prime,
So in July 2013, based on a panel of soccer experts, *World Soccer* listed midfielder Diego Maradona as a member of its Greatest XI of All Time.

In 2014, due to a vote by its readers from around the world, a soccer news website would proclaim:
Diego Maradona's induction as a charter member of the Goal Hall of Fame.

On 1/19/15, from the Italian Football Federation, Diego Maradona received much acclaim;
In the Best Foreign Player category, he was inducted into the Italian Football Hall of Fame.

In Argentina, Diego Maradona's superb coaching skills were heard and seen
When he was a mental coach for the Deportivo Riestra Asociación de Fomento Barrio Colón from 2013 to 2017.

A United Arab Emirates second-tier soccer team felt that Diego's intelligence was keen,
So he became the head coach of the Fujairah Football Club in 2017.

On 9/17/18, during his head-coaching debut for the host Club Dorados de Sinaloa, a professional soccer team based in Culiacán Rosales, Mexico, Diego Maradona continued to intrigue;
In an Ascenso MX contest, Maradona's team defeated the Cafetaleros de Tapachula Futbol Club 4-1, so he recorded his first win in Mexico's second-tier soccer league.

In 2019, a team in the Argentine First Division knew that Diego Maradona's head-coaching skills were still key,
So he became the manager of Argentina's Club de Gimnasia y Esgrima La Plata (La Plata Gymnastics and Fencing Club), simply known as CGE.

November 25, 2020, was a very sad day
Because Diego Maradona passed away.

Soccer fans around the world were in mourning, like fans in India who still remember Diego
Maradona's December 2017 trip to their country, which included a dedication in Kolkata of a 12-foot-
tall statue of Diego holding the 1986 World Cup championship trophy and also a soccer clinic in
Kadambagachi that he led for the children of Aditya School of Sports.
Two days after Diego Maradona passed away, on November 27, 2020, the same stadium where he
conducted that soccer workshop three years previously was renamed the Diego Maradona Aditya
School of Sports Cricket Stadium, which shows Diego Maradona had fans in towns and cities around
the world, and even in faraway ports and remote resorts.

Napoli officially renamed its stadium from Stadio San Paolo to Stadio Diego Armando Maradona on
December 4, 2020,
To honor his time on the team because his achievements were plenty.

For leading Argentina to the 1986 World Cup championship, Diego Maradona deserves a loud cheer.
He also scored an incredible 34 goals in 91 matches during his illustrious international career!

The United States Women's National Team

Superb soccer has long been played by terrific teammates who enjoyed each other's confidence, which sometimes led soccer teams to sporting dominance.
Nowadays, that includes the United States Women's National Team (USWNT) whose stellar performances over the last three decades has brought American soccer to global prominence!

In 1991, when the inaugural FIFA Women's World Cup was held in the People's Republic of China, the United States Women's National Team was divine.
Forwards April Dawn Heinrichs (captain), Carin Leslie Jennings, and Michelle Anne Akers-Stahl were known as the "Triple-Edged Sword Line."

On 11/24/91, at Foshan, China's New Plaza Stadium, Michelle Akers-Stahl found even greater fame When she set a record in Team USA's 7-0 win over Chinese Taipei by scoring five goals in a World Cup game!

On 11/30/91, at Guangzhou, China's Tianhe Stadium, in the World Cup Final, Michelle Akers-Stahl led Team USA:
She scored both of the United States' goals in a 2-1 contest, so America defeated Norway.

In the 1991 World Cup, Michelle Akers-Stahl set a Women's World Cup record for a single tournament with her 10 goals, so she was adored;
Since Michelle was the tournament's top goal scorer, she won the Golden Shoe Award.
Named the tournament's best player, Carin Jennings won the Golden Ball Award, so she was obviously a star and no sleeper.
Albert Anson Dorrance IV was Team USA's manager (head coach), and Mary Virginia Harvey stood strong (and moved quickly) as America's starting goalkeeper.
The People's Republic of China hosted this historic tournament, a world away from Philadelphia — the birthplace of this author — a city known to some simply as Philly.
Team USA also featured goalkeepers Amy Marie Allmann and Kimberlee Lynn "Kim" Maslin-Kammerdeiner; defenders Debbie Lynne Belkin, Joy Lynn Biefeld, Linda Ann Hamilton, Lori Ann Henry, and Carla Werden; forwards Brandi Denise Chastain and Wendy Sue Gebauer; and midfielders Tracey Marie Bates, Julie Maurine Foudy, Mariel Margaret "Mia" Hamm, Shannon Danise Higgins, and Kristine Marie Lilly.

The 1996 Summer Olympic Games held in Atlanta, Georgia — the first Olympics to ever feature women's soccer — listed Team USA's head coach as Anthony Dominick "Tony" DiCicco Jr. and America's starting goaltender as Briana Collette Scurry.
Not having reached the finals of global competition since its World Cup championship in 1991, this was a team playing hard and playing to win: a team in a hurry.
Team USA featured two very capable captains, midfielder Julie Foudy and defender Carla Overbeck (née Werden), whose leadership kept the competition in check.
The squad relied on great teamwork, inspired by an attitude of "all hands on deck."

On 8/1/96, at Sanford Stadium in Athens, Georgia, the Olympic Gold Medal Game between the United States of America and the People's Republic of China was a close 2-1 contest;

Yet midfielder Shannon Ann MacMillan and forward Tiffeny Carleen Milbrett each scored a goal that night — so in these Summer Games, Team USA proved to be the best.

That summer, the United States Women's National Team featured a full slate of sensational soccer stars able to successfully carry out a winning program,

Including goalies Mary Harvey and Saskia Johanna Webber; defenders Brandi Chastain, Joy Fawcett (née Biefeld), Thori Yvette Staples, and Staci Nicole Wilson; midfielders Kristine Lilly, Amanda Caryl Cromwell, Tiffany Marie Roberts, Jennifer White "Jen" Streiffer, Tisha Lea Venturini, and Michelle Akers (previously a forward); and forwards Carin Gabarra (née Jennings), Cynthia Marie "Cindy" Parlow, and Mia Hamm.

Team USA was all action, and its fans were never bored.

The squad also won the FIFA Fair Play Award.

American women were again divine,
In the World Cup tournament of 1999.
Tony DiCicco implemented an amazing approach
In his work as Team USA's head coach.

On 7/10/99, when facing the People's Republic of China, Briana Scurry successfully played her role As America's goalie in the World Cup Final at Pasadena, California's Rose Bowl.

That Brandi Chastain was a clutch defender, there was no doubt:

In a game still scoreless after overtime, she converted the decisive kick in a 5-4 penalty shootout!

Brandi Chastain celebrated when Team USA completed its successful trek.

The crew's captain again was defender Carla Overbeck.

This tournament encouraged many young girls to play soccer, and some of them even became pros.

Also, exactly twenty years later at the Rose Bowl, a statue was unveiled of Brandi Chastain's celebratory pose.

In 1999, the American women lived an international soccer dream:
Akers, Chastain, Hamm, Overbeck, and Scurry were named to the World Cup All-Star Team.
Having now won a third world championship in the decade — Olympic gold in 1996 and World Cups in 1991 and 1999 — the United States Women's National Team's popularity continued to grow.
Credit goes to the efforts of goalie Tracy Jean Ducar, defenders Christie Patricia Pearce and Kathryn Michele "Kate" Sobrero, midfielders Lorraine Ming "Lorrie" Fair and Sara Eve Whalen, forward Danielle Ruth Fotopoulos, and the aforementioned Fawcett, Foudy, Lilly, MacMillan, Milbrett, Roberts, Venturini, Webber, and Parlow.
On the field and and also in press interviews, the American women proved to be very skillful, intelligent, and quick.
They were becoming a media sensation, so on July 19, 1999, *Time*'s front cover featured Team USA and the punning caption "What a Kick!"

In 1999, the United States Olympic Committee (USOC) held Team USA as a group to revere,
So the women's national soccer squad was named the USOC Team of the Year.
Also, to put the icing on the cake, *Sports Illustrated* gave this soccer squad a compliment most sincere,
Proclaiming the United States Women's National Team to be the magazine's Sportswomen of the Year.

For the Summer Olympics in Athens, Greece, April Heinrichs — the 1991 World Cup captain and champion — was the head coach of the United States Women's National Team in 2004;
She greatly helped Chastain, Fair, Fawcett, Hamm, Lilly, MacMillan, Markgraf (née Sobrero), Parlow, Rampone (née Pearce), Roberts, Scurry, and team captain Julie Foudy, so the Americans continued to soar.

On 8/26/04, Team USA's performance in another Olympic Gold Medal Game, another 2-1 contest, was a thrill;
Midfielder Lindsay Ann Tarpley and forward Mary Abigail "Abby" Wambach each scored a goal when the United States beat Brazil.
The United States Women's National Team also featured goalies Kristin Stewart Luckenbill and Hope Amelia Solo, defenders Heather Blaine Mitts and Catherine Anne "Cat" Reddick, forward Heather Ann O'Reilly, and midfielders Angela Khalia Hucles, Alyson Kay "Aly" Wagner, and Shannon Leigh Boxx.
In other notable sporting news that year, the fabled "Curse of the Bambino" was finally lifted when, after 85 Major League Baseball (MLB) seasons of futility, the World Series was won again by the Boston Red Sox.

In the People's Republic of China, the United States Women's National Team continued to play great
When Pia Mariane Sundhage was its head coach at the first Olympic Games ever held in China —
Summer or Winter — the Summer Olympics of 2008.

On 8/21/08, the Olympic Gold Medal Game between the United States of America and Brazil was much enjoyed,
Though the only goal of the contest was scored in overtime by American midfielder Carli Anne Lloyd.

In the 2008 Summer Olympics, Kate Markgraf and Christie Rampone were like two peas in a pod
Because they were two terrific defenders and the co-captains of the American squad.
Over the course of the Olympic tournament, the Americans won every battle of wits, so their opponents experienced many fits.
The roster that summer included goalies Nicole Renee Barnhart and Briana Scurry; forwards Lauren Nicole Cheney, Natasha Kanani Janine Kai, and Amy Joy Rodriguez; midfielders Shannon Boxx, Angela Hucles, Heather O'Reilly (previously a forward), Lindsay Tarpley, and Kacey Dell White; and defenders Rachel Marie Buehler, Lori Christine Chalupny, Stephanie Renee Cox, Alexandra Blaire "Ali" Krieger, India Ashlei Trotter, and Heather Mitts.
Midfielders Tobin Powell Heath and Aly Wagner were also team members and each a terrific pro,
Yet the Woman of the Match was the United States' goalie, the appropriately named Hope Solo.

On 8/9/12, in yet another Olympic Gold Medal Game, this time at London, England's Wembley Stadium, Team USA's performance was again very bold, as this squad was still in its prime.
In another classic 2-1 match, with both goals contributed by midfielder Carli Lloyd, the United States beat Japan, taking the Olympic gold home to America for a third consecutive time!
Carli Lloyd became the first and only soccer player — female or male — in two consecutive Olympic Finals to score *both* game-winning goals.
Carli Lloyd, a Philly sports fan, cheered for the Philadelphia Eagles' new quarterback that same year — later named the Most Valuable Player (MVP) of Super Bowl LII — Nicholas Edward "Nick" Foles!
The Japanese women would kick but American goalie Hope Solo would catch;
Carli Lloyd's outstanding offensive performance got her named the Woman of the Match.
In addition, head coach Pia Sundhage and captain Christie Rampone executed a victorious plan,
So the United States Women's National Team defeated Japan.

In the 2012 Summer Olympic Games, Boxx, Buehler, Cheney, Heath, Mitts, O'Reilly, Rodriguez, and Wambach showed a lot of heart and played very smart,
As did forwards Sydney Rae Leroux, Alexandra Patricia "Alex" Morgan, and Christen Annemarie Press; midfielders Meghan Elizabeth Klingenberg, Lori Ann Lindsey, and Megan Anna Rapinoe; defenders Amy Elizabeth LePeilbet, Kelley Maureen O'Hara, and Rebecca Elizabeth "Becky" Sauerbrunn; and goalies Jillian Ann Loyden and Nicole Barnhart.

In 2012, Pia Sundhage and Abby Wambach kept their cool and showed no fear;
So, respectively, for women's soccer, they were named the FIFA World Coach of the Year and the FIFA World Player of the Year.

Jillian Anne "Jill" Ellis became the latest engine to drive Team USA's soccer machine
When she was named the squad's head coach in 2014.

On 6/16/15, at Vancouver, British Columbia's BC Place Stadium in Canada, forward Abby Wambach set a United States record with her 14th career World Cup goal, the only goal of the game, so Team USA beat Nigeria;
Abby Wambach also set a World Cup record with her 12th match of scoring at least one goal; this record was later matched in 2019 by Brazil's Marta Vieira da Silva, so both players met this standard of soccer superstar criteria.

On 7/5/15, back at BC Place Stadium, at only 2:34 into the World Cup Final between America and Japan, midfielder Carli Lloyd scored the fastest goal in a Women's World Cup Final ever: she ran down the field and threaded her way through the defensive holes, as her teammates fulfilled their roles. Carli Lloyd's third goal in the 16th minute of the contest completed the quickest hat trick in World Cup history — it was a chip shot from around midfield and was later named the Goal of the Tournament — and she also set a World Cup Final record with her three first-half goals!

This wonderful World Cup Final between America and Japan was full of exciting goals, assists, saves, and catches.

Carli Lloyd set two Women's World Cup records: three goals in a *single* Final match and a grand total of three goals in *all* Final matches.

Carli Lloyd would earn a tournament-best fourth (consecutive) Live Your Goals Player of the Match honor, because she matched the record set in 1966 by England's Geoffrey Charles "Geoff" Hurst with a World Cup Final hat trick.

In the World Cup Final between America and Japan, the Americans were extremely enthusiastic, energetic, and quick.

In addition to Carli Lloyd's history-making hat trick, one goal each was scored by midfielders Lauren Holiday (née Cheney; the wife of guard Jrue Randall Holiday, who later helped the Milwaukee Bucks win the 2020-2021 National Basketball Association championship) and Tobin Heath, to add to Japan's dismay.

America prevailed 5-2, and only three years after the Olympic outcome, with a repeat of the defeat of Japan in a world championship final, the Americans again had their way!

Setting two Women's World Cup records of her own, captain Christie Rampone deserved much praise: She became the oldest player ever to appear in a Final and the oldest champion, at the incredible age of 40 years and 11 days.

Carli Lloyd was born in New Jersey, just over the Pennsylvania state line, so she grew up cheering for the Philadelphia Phillies, the MLB team based in "The City of Brotherly Love."

It was no surprise that the 2015 World Cup honors included Carli Lloyd's award for the best player, the Golden Ball, and Hope Solo's award for the best goalie, the Golden Glove.

In the 2015 World Cup, Krieger, Lloyd, Morgan, Rapinoe, Solo, and defender Julie Beth Johnston were held in high esteem:
So, for the tournament, these six standout players were all named to FIFA's Dream Team.
Four of these six — Johnston, Lloyd, Rapinoe, and Solo — would get an additional nod,
Along with defender Meghan Klingenberg (previously a midfielder), in being selected to the FIFA Technical Study Group's All-Star Squad.

In the 2015 World Cup, Boxx, Chalupny, Leroux, O'Hara, O'Reilly, Rodriguez, Sauerbrunn, and Wambach were a success,
Along with goalies Ashlyn Michelle Harris and Alyssa Michele Naeher, defender Whitney Elizabeth Engen, midfielder Morgan Paige Brian, and forward Christen Press.

The 2015 World Cup title — Team USA's *seventh* world championship in 25 years — was the result of on-field performances that were gritty;
Therefore, on 7/10/15, a ticker-tape parade was thrown for the team in the streets of "The Big Apple," New York City.

Even in the bright lights of the global stage, the United States Women's National Team reigned supreme;
So, on 7/15/15, the American squad won the Excellence in Sports Performance Yearly (ESPY) award for the Best Team.

In 2015, Carli Lloyd was named the Philadelphia Sports Writers Association's Athlete of the Year, so she deserved a loud cheer.
Another honor was bestowed upon Team USA when the 2015 squad was named *Sports Illustrated*'s Inspiration of the Year.
For women's soccer, the World Coach of the Year and the World Player of the Year were Jill Ellis and Carli Lloyd, respectively, so they stood tall;
These two honorary titles were awarded to them by FIFA, whose full name in English is translated as "International Federation of Association Football."

On 6/11/19, in its World Cup opener at Reims, France's Stade Auguste-Delaune, Team USA's 13-0 win was grand, perhaps even *too* grand:

America's number of goals and its margin of victory set World Cup single-game records when it routed Thailand!

Clearly, this World Cup contest between the United States of America and Thailand was a *mis*match.

Captain Alex Morgan, a striker, scored five goals to tie the World Cup single-game record — a record set in 1991 by America's Michelle Akers-Stahl and matched in 1994 by Russia's Oleg Anatolyevich Salenko — as the Americans beat the Thai team with dispatch!

Because Team USA's teamwork was very nice,

Midfielders Rosemary Kathleen "Rose" Lavelle and Samantha June Mewis each scored twice.

The other two team captains, forwards Carli Lloyd and Megan Rapinoe (both of whom were midfielders in the previous World Cup), also showed great ball control:

Along with midfielder Lindsey Michelle Horan and forward Mallory Diane Pugh, they each scored a goal.

For their outstanding offensive performance, the Americans deserved much acclaim;

They set a record with their seven different goal scorers for a Women's World Cup game.

The Americans became a big part of World Cup lore;

With seven different goal scorers, they tied the World Cup single-game record set by Yugoslavia in 1974.

On 6/16/19, at Paris, France's Parc des Princes, when Team USA beat Chile, unhappy South American soccer fans certainly had several good reasons to pout:

Carli Lloyd scored two goals and midfielder Julie Ertz (née Johnston; previously a defender) scored one goal, plus the Americans played dynamic defense, so the team recorded a 3-0 shutout.

In the 11th minute, the consistent Carli Lloyd would again accurately aim,

Setting yet another Women's World Cup record by scoring in a sixth consecutive game.

For its second goal of the match, the United States of America would depend

On Julie Ertz, the wife of the Philadelphia Eagles' Zachary Adam "Zach" Ertz — who in Super Bowl LII scored the game-winning touchdown with an 11-yard catch, cementing his legacy as a clutch tight end!

At the time of this international competition, 36 years and 11 months was Carli Lloyd's age;

She became the oldest player ever to score more than one goal in a Women's World Cup game — soccer's biggest stage.

On 6/20/19, at Le Havre, France's Stade Océane, Team USA beat Sweden 2-0 in a World Cup contest that was talked about
Because Lindsey Horan scored a goal and midfielder-turned-forward Tobin Heath's superb shot was deflected and recorded as an own goal, when the squad earned its third consecutive shutout.

In the 2019 World Cup, while recording three straight shutouts, America's soccer intelligence was keen;
For goals in a group stage of three games, Team USA set the World Cup record with an astonishing 18.

The United States Women's National Team had dominated its opponents in three straight matches because, under head coach Jill Ellis, the players were able to effectively train.
On 6/24/19, back at Stade Auguste-Delaune, in a round-of-16 contest, Megan Rapinoe scored twice by converting two penalty kicks to power America's 2-1 victory over Spain.

On 6/28/19, back at Parc des Princes, in a World Cup quarterfinal contest, Megan Rapinoe took advantage of each chance,
So she scored both American goals in a 2-1 contest when Team USA beat France.
Megan became the first player in Women's World Cup history to score two goals in consecutive elimination games, and she did so by exploiting defensive holes.
Over these two close contests, Rapinoe also became the first United States player ever to score four consecutive Women's World Cup goals.

On 7/2/19, at France's Stade de Lyon, in a World Cup semifinal match against England, United States goalkeeper Alyssa Naeher was slick:
For a Women's World Cup contest, she became the first U.S. goalie in regulation time to save a penalty kick!
With a sixth consecutive win and a third consecutive 2-1 victory, the Americans again had their way.
Forward Christen Press scored the opening goal of the game, and Alex Morgan became the first player in a Women's World Cup contest to score a goal (the game-winner) on her (30th) birthday.

On 7/7/19, back at Stade de Lyon, in the World Cup Final against the Netherlands, the United States Women's National Team got its first score
When Megan Rapinoe converted a second-half penalty kick, becoming the oldest player to score a goal in a Women's World Cup Final, at the age of 34.
A second goal to seal America's 2-0 victory was scored later in the half by Rose Lavelle.
The Americans had also set a World Cup record with their 12th consecutive win, as their teamwork continued to jell.

In the 2019 World Cup tournament, Megan played in only five of America's seven games but still recorded six goals and three assists, so her performances would enthrall.
As the leading goal scorer of the World Cup, Rapinoe won the Golden Boot Award, and as the tournament's top player, she won another award, the Golden Ball.
Team USA set a record for a single Women's World Cup tournament with 26 goals, greatly helped by Jill Ellis' sage advice.
Ellis also became both the second head coach (Italy's Vittorio Pozzo was the first to achieve this feat, in 1934 and 1938) — and the first *women's* head coach ever — to win the World Cup twice.
Defender Crystal Alyssia Dunn, Julie Ertz, Rose Lavelle, and Megan Rapinoe gave performances that were especially fine,
So these four players were named to the FIFA Technical Study Group's list of Players Who Dared to Shine.

In the 2019 World Cup tournament, from their opening match to the Final match, the Americans were consistently strong;
Five other players on the team were forward Jessica Marie McDonald, goalies Adrianna Nichole Franch and Ashlyn Harris, and midfielders Morgan Brian and Alexandra Linsley "Allie" Long.
Despite a history of winning championships, the Americans weren't jaded at all; they remained energetic and eager.
Six other players on the team were defenders Abigail Lynn "Abby" Dahlkemper, Tierna Lillis Davidson, Emily Ann Sonnett, Kelley O'Hara, Becky Sauerbrunn, and Ali Krieger.

On 7/10/19, events honoring Team USA, on both American coasts, celebrated that Wednesday's theme:
First, with a New York City ticker-tape parade, and then in Los Angeles with an ESPY award for the Best Team.
Watching Alex Morgan excel in the 2019 World Cup was a real treat,
So she was honored with an ESPY award for the Best Female Athlete.

Jill Ellis was named The Best FIFA Women's Coach of 2019 because her leadership skills were extraordinary, like a great city's mayor.
Also for 2019, Megan Rapinoe was named as one of the *Glamour* Women of the Year and also named as The Best FIFA Women's Player.
On soccer's biggest stage, while leading Team USA to the 2019 World Cup title, Megan Rapinoe would repeatedly score.
Since Megan was named the best female soccer player of 2019 by the magazine *France Football*, she won its Women's Ballon d'Or Award, cementing her place in international soccer lore.

In 2019, *Sports Illustrated* was, as ever, entertaining, informative, wise, witty, and clear;
So it was no surprise when the magazine named Megan Rapinoe its Sportsperson of the Year.
Tennis star Christine Marie "Chris" Evert (1976), track star Mary Teresa Decker (1983), tennis star Serena Jameka Williams (2015), and soccer star Megan Rapinoe (2019) are all deservedly well known;
In addition to all of their other athletic achievements, they are also the only four women to ever win this supreme *Sports Illustrated* award as an individual on their own.

Though the United States Women's National Team has always been too humble to boast,
For women's soccer competitions, the team's four World Cup championships and four Olympic gold medals are the most!

Sources

Rhymes were checked with and inspired by the RhymeZone website.

Other websites consulted include the following: FIFA, Goal (a soccer news website), the official website of Diego Armando Maradona, the official Facebook page of Pelé, U.S. Soccer, and Wikipedia.

Publications used include the following: the *San Francisco Chronicle*, *Sports Illustrated*, *The Philadelphia Inquirer*, and *The Press of Atlantic City.*

Acknowledgments

Thanks to Bob Rigby for writing a fabulous foreword.

Thanks to Keir Radnedge for answering my questions about Pelé and for contributing a back cover quote.

Thanks to Chuck Nan for thoroughly answering my research questions.

Thanks to Scott Werner for his excellent editorial work.

Thanks to Ryan Kerrigan for his awesome artwork.

Thanks to my brother David Auday for the 1975 Philadelphia Wings program page and also to the Philadelphia Wings for giving me permission to use it in this book.

Thanks to Alton Scott Muhammad for editing three photos.

Thanks to Susan Penner for her technological assistance.

Thanks to Eddie Blume and Dan Pitkow for answering my questions about our youth soccer team, the Penn Valley Mustangs.

About the Author

Paul James Auday graduated from Harriton High School in Rosemont, Pennsylvania. He earned bachelor's and master's degrees and an administrative credential from the University of California, Berkeley, as well as a teaching credential from Metropolitan State College of Denver. Currently, Mr. Auday is an elementary school teacher in the San Francisco Bay Area. His website, which features many unique videos with sports stars, is www.sportsrhymes.com.

Printed in the United States
by Baker & Taylor Publisher Services